LAB series

# GARDENING LAB
## FOR KIDS

## Garden Art

### FUN EXPERIMENTS TO LEARN, GROW, HARVEST, MAKE, AND PLAY

RENATA FOSSEN BROWN

QUARRY

**Quarto Knows**

Inspiring | Educating | Creating | Entertaining

Brimming with creative inspiration, how-to projects, and useful information to enrich your everyday life, Quarto Knows is a favorite destination for those pursuing their interests and passions. Visit our site and dig deeper with our books into your area of interest: Quarto Creates, Quarto Cooks, Quarto Homes, Quarto Lives, Quarto Drives, Quarto Explores, Quarto Gifts, or Quarto Kids.

Content for this book was originally found in *Gardening Lab for Kids* by Renata Fossen Brown (Quarry Books, 2014)

Cover Image: Dave Brown
Photography: Dave Brown
Illustration: Renata Fossen Brown

Printed in China

MIX
Paper from
responsible sources
FSC® C008080

# ✳ CONTENTS ✳

# * INTRODUCTION *

It's been said that "gardening is better than therapy and you get tomatoes." I would agree. Gardening is also the combination of art and science. This book is a collection of activities I've used both professionally at Cleveland Botanical Garden and personally during the past twenty years. To me, gardening is everything good: exercise (but more fun), being outside (usually), communing with nature, and (hopefully) bettering a tiny patch of earth. I'm not a professional gardener, I'm not a horticulturist, but I do hang out with a bunch of them and ask a lot of questions. The biggest thing I've learned through these interactions is that all of those "rules" they learned in school are simply there to be broken.

Gardening is a personal endeavor, and whatever makes you happy should be what you do. If you love putting pinks and oranges together because they make you smile, then do it. If, instead of the rules of three, you prefer groups of four, then do it.

I get great ideas of things to do in my yard from daily walks with the dogs, plant catalogs, and Pinterest! From these same three places, I also see plenty of things I don't want in my yard. Either way, you learn new things to implement—or not.

# * GARDEN ART *

Gardens are, by their very nature, works of art. Many art concepts, such as texture, line, symmetry, color, and focal point are used when designing garden spaces. Additionally, gardens are perfect places to display works of art. Beautiful backdrops of shrubs, trees, and flowers are only enhanced when an artistic creation is placed amid them. This unit will have you getting creative with paint, water, cement, and bottle caps to make unique items for your outdoor space. The messier you get, the better.

## * MATERIALS *

→ Recycled plastic carryout containers no bigger than 1' (30 cm) across

→ Vegetable oil

→ Decorative stone or gravel, or marbles, etc.

→ Tub or bucket for mixing cement

→ Bag of perlite

→ Bag of peat moss

→ Bag of Portland cement

→ Dust mask

→ Rubber gloves

→ Plastic wrap

*NOTE: Always wear a dust mask when working with these materials, and always wear gloves when mixing these materials together.*

**Making your own stepping stones is an easy way of personalizing your garden.** By using containers that were going to be thrown into the recycling bin anyway, you are saving the planet while saving money.

## * DIG IN! *

*Fig. 1: Apply oil to the container.*

*Fig. 2: Place decorative stones.*

Fig. 3: Mix the perlite, peat moss, and cement together.

Fig. 4: Add water to the mixture and mix with your hands.

Fig. 5: Scoop and press the mixture into each container.

1. Cover the insides of the containers with vegetable oil. This will help the hardened stepping stones pop out of the containers. (Fig. 1)

2. Place decorative stones or marbles into the container. (Fig. 2)

3. Mix equal parts perlite, peat moss, and Portland cement in a tub or bucket. Break up any chunks and wear a dust mask while doing this. (Fig. 3)

4. Wear gloves and slowly add water to the mixture, stirring with your hands. Ultimately you want it to be the consistency of cottage cheese—not too dry, not too wet. (Fig. 4)

5. Carefully scoop the mixture into each container, on top of the stones or gravel. Press the mixture down to push out any air bubbles. Cover the containers with plastic wrap for three to four days to cure. After several days, unwrap a stone and try pressing your fingernail into it. If you can't make an indentation, then it is ready to carefully remove from the container. (Fig. 5)

## ✳ DIG DEEPER! ✳

### CARING FOR YOUR STEPPING STONES

→ The mixture used in this Lab, called hypertufa, takes several weeks to completely cure, so keep the stepping stones out of direct sunlight until then. While they cure, misting them with water regularly helps strengthen and prevent them from cracking.

→ If you live where winter temperatures are below freezing, bring your stepping stones inside during the cold months to extend their life.

## * MATERIALS *

→ 42 metal bottle caps

→ Piece of scrap wood

→ Scratch awl
(or a roofing nail)

→ Hammer

→ ⅛" (3 mm) wide ribbon

→ Tapestry needle

→ Plastic lid from coffee
container

→ 7 buttons or beads

→ Metal twist tie

**Wind chimes are whimsical ornaments that add pleasant sounds and movement to your garden.**
Making them is fun and allows for lots of creativity in the materials you use. Here we are using some upcycling items that otherwise may have been thrown away. Before starting, arrange your materials on a flat surface and lay out newspaper.

## \\|||||| * DIG IN! * ||||||/

1. Place bottle caps upside down on the piece of scrap wood. Aim the awl or nail at the rubber seal and hammer it into the cap to punch a hole. Remove the awl and continue with each bottle cap. (Fig. 1)

2. Cut seven 36" (91 cm) pieces of ribbon. Using the tapestry needle, thread the ribbon through the hole on a bottle cap and tie a double knot just above the cap to keep it in place. (Fig. 2)

3. Continue adding five more bottle caps at different spacing along the length of the ribbon. Leave 6" (15 cm) of ribbon at the end. (Fig. 3)

4. Use the awl to punch holes into the plastic lid. Once you have seven lengths of ribbon threaded with caps, thread each ribbon through a hole in the plastic lid, knotting the ribbon once through a button or bead to hold it in place. (Fig. 4)

5. Gather all of the loose ends of ribbon together and wrap the metal twist tie around them to their ends. Wrap it around on itself to form a loop and secure the ends. (Fig. 5)

Fig. 1: Punch holes in the bottle caps.

Fig. 2: Thread and knot the ribbon.

Fig. 3: Add more caps to the ribbon.

Fig. 4: Thread the ribbon through the plastic lid and knot it.

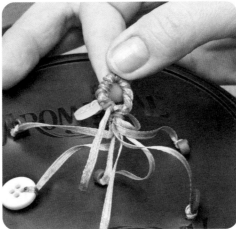

Fig. 5: Wrap the twist tie around the loose ribbon ends.

## ✴ DIG DEEPER! ✴
### UPCYCLING

Upcycling is an environmental way of reusing otherwise useless materials and turning them into something functional. Look around for other materials you could upcycle and use in your garden. What are some things you normally throw away or recycle that you could use? Start a garden journal and keep a list of items for possible projects.

## * MATERIALS *

→ Large lids from glass jars

→ Scratch awl

→ Permanent marker

→ Wire hangers

→ Needle nose pliers

**Once your garden is growing and full of gorgeous greenery, people will want to know the names of every plant in it.** You will probably remember many, if not all, but sometimes we just plain forget. Make and display these upcycled plant labels so people can see what you are growing. Learn a little Latin while you're at it, too.

*Fig. 1: Poke two holes in each lid.*

## * DIG IN! *

1. Use the scratch awl to make a hole in the inside edge of a lid. This will be the top of the plant label. Poke another hole on the opposite side (the bottom) to allow water to drain out. (Fig. 1)

2. Using the permanent marker, write the common name of a plant in the center of the inside of a lid. If you also know the Latin name of the plant, write that along the bottom of the lid. (Fig. 2)

3. Straighten the wire hanger. Use the pliers to cut it into three equal segments. (Fig. 3)

4. Loop the wire through the top of the top hole. Wrap the wire around the back of the lid so the lid hangs from it. Push the wire into the ground near the plant and you're ready for garden tours! (Fig. 4)

Fig. 2: Write the plant name on the lid.

Fig. 3: Cut the hanger into three equal pieces.

Fig. 4: Insert wire into the lid.

# ✳ DIG DEEPER! ✳
## LEARN SOME LATIN

→ Oh Latin names, how I love thee. All living things in the universe have a Latin name that consists of two words. Human beings are called *Homo sapiens*, which translates to "wise man." All Latin names are italicized and the first word is always capitalized. The first word is the *genus*, the second is the *species*.

→ Organisms are given a scientific or Latin name so that each living thing has only one correct name. If you are in Ohio talking about *Echinacea purpurea*, your friend in Belgium knows you're looking at the Eastern purple coneflower.

→ Scientific names differ from common names in that every organism has only one scientific name but may have many common names. For example, *Actaea simplex* is also commonly known as baneberry, snakeroot, purple snakeroot, autumn bugbane, black cohosh, bugbane, and autumn snakeroot!

→ Here are just a handful of Latin roots and their meanings. The next time you read a plant label at a nursery, you'll know more about the plant from its name if any of these are a part of it:

*Alba* – white
*Acer* – sharp
*Crassula* - thick
*Barbata* – bearded, hairy
*Dura* – hard
*Echinos* – hedgehog, porcupine
*Eros* – love, heart-shaped
*Eximia* – excellent

*Flavus* – yellow
*Ferox* – strongly armed with teeth (Yikes!)
*Glabrus* – smooth
*Magna* – big
*Rubra* – red
*Vulgaris* – common

# SOUP CAN LUMINARIES

## * MATERIALS *

→ Empty soup can, label removed

→ Old towel

→ Scratch awl

→ Hammer

→ 18 gauge wire

*Tip: If you do not want to use these as hangers, fill the bottom of each can with 1" (2.5cm) of sand to add weight and prevent them from blowing over when there is a candle inside.*

**Lanterns and luminaries are ancient ways of lighting spaces.** The early Greeks and Romans used them to see at night and provide some security. A luminary is defined as "a body that gives off light." It can also be defined as "an important person of prominence and achievement." So when you complete this Lab, can you be called a "Luminary Luminary"?

## * DIG IN! *

1. Fill the can with water and place in the freezer overnight. This step makes it easier to poke holes into the sides of the can without the can collapsing into itself. Don't leave it in there much longer as the can may split open. (Fig. 1)

2. Remove the can from the freezer. Lay it on its side on the folded up towel. The towel will help hold the can in place while you work. (Fig. 2)

3. Use the scratch awl and hammer to poke two holes at the top of each can directly across from each other. These will be used for hanging the luminaries. (Fig. 3)

4. Starting 1" (2.5 cm) from the bottom of the can, carefully use the scratch awl and hammer to pound holes randomly all over the can. (Fig. 4)

5. Loop the wire through the two holes at the top for hanging. (Fig. 5)

Fig. 1: Fill the can with water and freeze.

Fig. 2: Lay the can on its side on the towel.

Fig. 3: Make openings at the top of the can for hanging.

Fig. 4: Hold the awl above the can and hit the base of it with the hammer to make holes.

Fig. 5: Loop the wire through the top holes and secure it.

# DIG DEEPER!
## LUMINARY TIPS

→ Use tealights in your luminaries, and never leave them unattended when lit. Use only with adult supervision or battery run lights.

→ Did you know some plants are flammable? Pines, junipers, and firs are very flammable, and open flame should not be used near them.

→ Draw a design on the cans with a grease pencil, then poke holes in the can following the design. When done, wipe the excess grease pencil markings off.

## * MATERIALS *

→ 4' (122 cm) sections of bamboo or similar wooden sticks

→ Rubber band

→ Colorful twine

→ Dandelion weeder or similar metal pokey thing

→ Sweet pea seeds

**Sure, you can buy a cheap boring trellis for your climbing plants to explore.** But even better is making your own fun structure for these cute flowers. If you were a sweet pea, wouldn't you want to climb up this?

## * DIG IN! *

1. Gather the bamboo sticks and keep them together by wrapping the rubber band around them three to four times until tight, about 3" (7.5 cm) from the ends of the sticks. Wrap the twine around the rubber band, covering it completely. (Fig. 1)

2. Spread the other ends of the bamboo out in a circle in the location you'll be planting the seeds. Use the dandelion weeder to poke holes in the ground for the sticks. Push the sticks firmly into the soil—you don't want it to come crashing down while your flowers are growing! (Fig. 2)

3. Plant two to three seeds at the base of each pole, following package directions, and water them in well. (Fig. 3)

Fig. 1: Wrap the rubber band around the bamboo. Then wrap the twine.

Fig. 2: Arrange the ends of the sticks into a circle.

Fig. 3: Plant and water your seeds.

# ✳ DIG DEEPER! ✳

## SEED COATS OF ARMOR

Fig. 4: Soak sweet pea seeds before planting.

→ Seeds are protected by an outer layer called the seed coat. Seed coats protect the inner baby plant from drying out and injury. To soften the outer seed coat for your sweet peas, soak them in water for several hours before planting (Fig. 4). When you are ready to plant them, the seed coat should be soft enough for you to lightly scratch it open with a fingernail or stick, allowing water and nutrients to enter the seed and begin growth.

→ Some seed coats are so strong they have to pass through the stomach acids of animals or live through a forest fire for the seed to grow!

# HYPERTUFA PLANTER

## * MATERIALS *

→ Plastic containers of various shapes and sizes, some large, some smaller

→ Vegetable oil

→ Bag of perlite

→ Bag of Portland cement

→ Bag of peat moss

→ Bucket or other large container

→ Dust mask

→ Rubber gloves

→ Plastic straw

→ Scissors

→ Plastic wrap

*NOTE: Always wear a dust mask when working with these materials and gloves when mixing them together.*

**For this Lab, use containers that nest inside one another so there is less than an inch (2.5 cm) in between them.** Let's call the bigger container in each pair the "nester" and the smaller one the "nestee."

##  * DIG IN! *

1. For each pair of containers, oil the inside of each nester and the outside of each nestee. This will help you remove the hardened hypertufa from the container. (Fig. 1)

2. Add equal parts perlite, cement, and peat moss to the bucket. Wear a dust mask and gloves and mix together using your hands. Break up any big clumps and remove any sticks. (Fig. 2)

3. Slowly add water to the mixture and carefully mix it with your hands (still wearing a mask and gloves!). Your end product should be smooth and not very wet. (Fig. 3)

4. Scoop some hypertufa mixture into the bottom of one of the nesters, so that it is about 1" (2.5 cm) deep. Cut a length from the plastic straw the same height and press it into the center of the mixture. This will be the drainage hole once you remove the straw after drying. (Fig. 4)

5. Insert the smaller container into the bigger, slightly pressing into the hypertufa mixture at the bottom. Scoop more hypertufa in between the two containers, filling to the top of the inner container. Smooth the top surface. (Fig. 5)

6. Cover each set of containers with plastic wrap. Remove the nestees the next day. Let them dry or "cure" for several more days. The plastic wrap helps hold in moisture so that the hypertufa dries slowly and strong. If you can scrape into the mixture with your fingernail, let it sit longer. (Fig. 6)

Fig. 1: Oil the containers.

Fig. 2: Mix the perlite, cement, and peat moss with your hands.

Fig. 3: Add water and mix.

Fig. 4: Add hypertufa mixture to the container. Press a straw into the center.

Fig. 5: Place the nestee into the nester and add hypertufa mixture.

Fig. 6: Cover the containers for several days.

# ✳ DIG DEEPER! ✳
## LOSE THE LIME!

When your hypertufa containers are completely cured (which, depending on their size, could take several weeks to several months), submerge them in water for several days to remove some of the lime in them from the cement. Large quantities of lime aren't good for plants.

## * MATERIALS *

→ Shallow bowl or dish

→ Waterproof silicone

→ Candlestick

**Let your creative juices roll for this activity!** Visit garage sales or thrift stores to buy crazy bowls and candlesticks very cheaply. It's fun to completely mismatch styles and be as imaginative as you want. These can also make great gifts!

*Fig. 1: Gather your materials.*

## * DIG IN! *

1. Cover your work surface and lay out your materials. Lay your bowl upside down on the table. (Fig. 1)

2. Squeeze a line of silicone completely around the top of the candlestick. Make sure it is a continuous bead of silicone so you have a complete, watertight seal when it dries. (Fig. 2)

Fig. 2: Line the top of the candlestick with the silicone.

Fig. 3: Press the candlestick to the bowl and let it dry.

Fig. 4: Enjoy your birdbath!

3. Press the candlestick onto the center of the bottom of the bowl. Let this dry upside down overnight. (Fig. 3)

4. Once completely dry, place the birdbath in your garden and fill with water for your birds to enjoy! Replace the water every other day so your birds have fresh, clean water. (Fig. 4)

# DIG DEEPER!

## BIRD FACTS

→ Did you know birds can't sweat? Flopping around in your birdbath will help keep them cool during the hot days of summer. Also, birds need to keep their feathers clean and in perfect condition so they can fly.

→ Birds aren't all that crazy about new things, so it may take them a couple of weeks to start enjoying their birdbath. Place it near a bird feeder or a shrub they congregate in. This may help them get accustomed to their new work of art sooner.

→ Depending on what your birdbath is made of, it probably cannot withstand winter cold without cracking. Remember to bring it inside when temperatures are expected to be below 32°F (0°C).

## * MATERIALS *

→ Newspapers for the work surface

→ Acrylic paints in several different colors

→ Paper plate

→ Natural paint sponges

→ Clay pots (We used 2" to 4" [5 to 10 cm] pots, but you can pick any size you want.)

→ Fun paper

→ Line of poetry or a saying you like

→ Water-based sealer (Mod Podge works well)

→ Foam brushes

→ Polyurethane

**I love the color and look of plain, old clay pots. But sometimes you just want a little bit more zip.** This Lab unleashes your creativity to make lovely works of art for your garden or for gifts. Before starting, wipe any dust or dirt off of the pot using a damp paper towel and allow it to dry. Cover your work surface with newspaper.

## * DIG IN! *

1. Squirt two to four different colors of paint onto the paper plate. (Fig. 1)

2. Dip the sponge into the paint, then dab it onto the pot in lovely randomness. Leave lots of empty space. Repeat with the other colors, allowing drying time between coats. (Fig. 2)

3. Type up and print the saying you want on the pot. Rip the paper into a thin strip that will fit around the rim of the pot. Brush the water-based sealer onto the rim, apply the paper, then brush more sealer over the paper to seal it. Allow this to dry. (Fig. 3)

4. Apply the polyurethane sealer to the entire pot, inside and out, to prevent the paint from chipping or pealing. Allow to dry. (Fig. 4)

*Fig. 1: Dispense paint onto the plate.*

*Fig. 2: Sponge paint the pot.*

*Fig. 3: Print a saying on a thin strip of paper and affix it to the pot rim.*

*Fig. 4: Seal the pot with polyurethane.*

# * DIG DEEPER! *

## MAKE A CLEVER WEDDING FAVOR

I know someone who made these pots for wedding favors. She had a lovely Native American proverb, along with the couple's wedding date, on the piece of paper on the rim. Because it was a fall wedding, she bought tons of crocus bulbs (her favorite), wrapped them in burlap, tied them with twine, and put each bundle into a pot. Oh, yeah! That was me.

## * MATERIALS *

→ Photos of bugs

→ Smooth rocks in different shapes and sizes

→ Pencil

→ Acrylic paint in all sorts of colors

→ Small paintbrushes

→ Polyurethane

→ Foam brush

**Bugs are important to have in the garden: they pollinate, protect biodiversity, eat bad things, and are themselves food for other things.** In this Lab, we pay homage to these delightful little creatures by making rock images of them to adorn your garden. You can be as realistic or fanciful with your creations as you wish. Find photos of bugs online or get some bug identification books from the library.

## * DIG IN! *

1. Make sure the rocks are clean and dry. Select the type of bug you want to paint and outline its design on the rock with pencil. (Fig. 1)

2. Use the paint to fill in the design. Allow paint to dry overnight. (Fig. 2)

3. Cover the entire design with the polyurethane to preserve your creation. Allow to dry. Place your rock bugs in your garden for everyone to admire. (Fig. 3)

Fig. 1: Draw the bug on the rock.

Fig. 2: Paint your bug and allow to dry.

Fig. 3: Coat your rock bug with polyurethane.

# DIG DEEPER!

## LEARN MORE ABOUT BUGS

→ When someone says the word *bugs*, he or she usually means any creepy crawly thing with a ton of legs. But by definition, an insect has six legs, three body parts, and a pair of antennae.

→ No one knows the exact number of different kinds of insects there are in the world. Estimates range from 1 million to 30 million.

→ The largest beetle in the world is from South America and is close to 8" (20 cm) long.

→ Dragonflies can fly 35 miles per hour (56 kph)!

→ Brightly colored insects may be warning others they are poisonous or dangerous if angered. Insects with muted colors are usually trying to blend in with their surroundings for protection.

**There is nothing more relaxing than the sounds of gurgling water.** Why not put this clay pot fountain together and enjoy the tranquility it brings to your garden? Make sure the pots are clean and dry before you start. Build your fountain next to the electrical outlet you'll use so you don't have to move it when you're done.

→ 5 clay pots in decreasing sizes, 12" to 6" (30 to 15 cm) approximately

→ Waterproofing repair tape

→ 3 ⅝" (16 mm) rubber leg tips

→ Waterproof silicone adhesive

→ Rubber tubing

→ Fountain pump

→ Small rocks, such as river rocks

## \* DIG IN! \*

1. Place the largest pot in the chosen location and use the waterproofing tape to cover the bottom drainage hole completely. Put the three rubber leg tips in the bottom of the pot equal distance from each other. Use the silicone to adhere them to the pot and allow this to dry overnight. (Fig. 1)

2. Attach the tubing to the fountain pump and place it on the bottom of the pot, in between the leg tips. Ensure the electrical cord is hanging outside the top of the base pot. (Fig. 2)

3. Place the third biggest pot upside down on top of the leg tips, threading the rubber tubing from the fountain pump through the hole. Use the waterproofing tape to seal the hole the tubing is coming out of. (Fig. 3)

Fig. 1: Tape the drainage hole and add the leg tips.

Fig. 2: Place the fountain pump above the drainage hole.

Fig. 3: Place pot inside largest pot, thread tubing through drainage hole, and seal.

4. Stack the biggest remaining pot right side up, on top of the upside down pot, and thread the tubing through the drainage holes. Seal the gaps with waterproofing tape. Continue this way until all five pots are used and the tubing is sticking out the top of the smallest pot. Begin adding the river rocks to the pots. Fill the pots with water and plug the pump into an electrical outlet to ensure it is working correctly. (Fig. 4)

NOTE: Make sure your hands and the fountain plug are completely dry before plugging into the outlet. Be careful when you do this as the water may come shooting straight up! Then fill the pots with the rocks, experimenting with placement for different water effects or sounds. Placing a larger rock near where the water comes out of the end of the tubing may be needed to slow the water flow if it is coming out too powerfully.

Fig. 4: Stack the pots until the smallest is on top with the fountain tubing sticking through. Seal each hole and add the river rock.

# ✳ DIG DEEPER! ✳

## ENJOY YOUR WATER FOUNTAIN

→ Before completely filling the fountain with the river rock, fill it with water and plug the pump in to ensure it is working. With all of the jostling it undergoes during the construction of the fountain, something may come dislodged. It's easier to remove a little bit of rock than if you had filled it completely.

→ The sound of bubbling water can mask other, unwanted sounds and create a lovely respite in your garden.

→ Moving water can attract birds, so place your bird feeder and birdbath (Lab 7) nearby.

# A PLACE TO REST

## * MATERIALS *

→ Scissors

→ 2" x 22" x 22" (5 x 56 x 56 cm) high-density foam

→ 4 yards (366 cm) outdoor fabric

→ Instant fabric and leather adhesive (Bish's Original Tear Mender works well)

→ 4 tree stumps

→ Polyurethane sealant and paint brush (optional)

**Stopping and smelling the roses is good for you, so you might as well have a nice place to sit while admiring your garden.** This project requires no sewing; just the skill to wrap a present.

## * DIG IN! *

1. Cut the foam into four equal pieces, each measuring 11" (28 cm) square. (Fig. 1)

2. Cut a piece of fabric so it is big enough to wrap around one piece of foam like you're wrapping a present. Trim excess fabric. (Fig. 2)

3. Use the adhesive to seal the edges of the fabric and let it dry according to product directions. Place your completed cushions on the tree stumps for a handy place to sit in your garden. (Fig. 3)

4. To protect the tree stumps, seal them with polyurethane and let them dry first.

Fig. 1: Cut the foam.

Fig. 2: Cut a piece of fabric to wrap around the foam.

Fig. 3: Seal the fabric edges.

# ✳ DIG DEEPER! ✳
## ENJOY NATURE

→ Once you find a nice spot to sit in your garden, close your eyes and breathe in and out slowly five times. As you inhale, imagine your lungs filling with good, clean air; when you exhale, concentrate on your heartbeat. Taking time each day to focus on your breathing can have very soothing and long-lasting effects.

→ As you sit in your garden, what sounds do you hear? Which sounds are from nature and which are man-made?

→ Can you smell what is blooming in your garden? How far from a bloom can you smell it?

# GRASSY GARDEN GNOMES

## * MATERIALS *

→ 1 pair knee-high nylons

→ Wide-mouth drinking glass

→ Spoon

→ Grass seed

→ Soil

→ Googly eyes

→ Waterproof glue, such as Gorilla Glue

→ Felt or foam pieces in various colors

→ Paint pens

→ Small clay pots

→ Small bowl

→ Small plastic or Styrofoam cups, such as Dixie cups

*Tip: This is a messy activity, so do this outside if you can. Otherwise spread newspaper on your work surface.*

**Fill your garden with gnomes to help watch over it and keep you company.**
Your garden gnome will be extra special as it will have actual growing "hair"!

## * DIG IN! *

1. Stretch one nylon stocking over the mouth of a wide drinking glass to make pouring the grass seed and soil into the nylon easy. Use a spoon to sprinkle a small handful of grass seed into the stocking. (Fig. 1)

2. Pour one to two handfuls of soil on top of the grass seed, pushing the soil all the way down to the toe. Take the nylon off of the drinking glass, and knot the nylon close to the soil to keep the soil in place. This is your gnome's head. (Fig. 2)

3. With the length of leftover nylon hanging downward, glue googly eyes onto the face area and add other facial features using the felt or foam pieces. Let the glue dry completely. Use the paint pens to paint the clay pots. (Fig. 3)

Fig. 1: Cover the mouth of a drinking glass.

Fig. 2: Pour soil on top of the grass seed, then knot the nylon stocking.

Fig. 3: Glue facial features on the gnome.

Fig. 4: Invert the gnome's head into the water.

Fig. 5: Insert the nylon "wick" into the cup.

4. Fill the bowl with water and invert the gnome's head into it for several minutes. This wets the soil and grass seed and gets the seed growing. (Fig. 4)

5. Insert a small paper cup into a clay pot and fill the cup with water. Flip the gnome's head right side up and insert the loose end of the nylon into the cup. The nylon will act as a wick to pull water up and keep the grass seed watered. Place the gnome where it will get sunlight, and within a week watch for the seed "hair" to sprout! (Fig. 5)

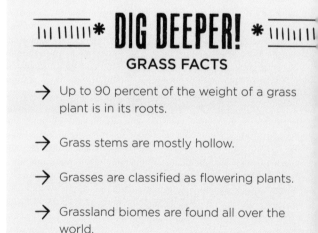

## ‖‖‖‖‖‖ * DIG DEEPER! * ‖‖‖‖‖‖
### GRASS FACTS

→ Up to 90 percent of the weight of a grass plant is in its roots.

→ Grass stems are mostly hollow.

→ Grasses are classified as flowering plants.

→ Grassland biomes are found all over the world.

# * RESURCES *

## Gardening Information

Heat zones in the United States:
**American Horticultural Society**
www.ahs.org

Outside the United States, find your hardiness zone here:
**www.backyardgardener.com/zone/#outside**

Order trees and get tons of useful information:
**Arbor Day Foundation**
www.arborday.org

List of plants that can be toxic to dogs and cats:
**The American Society for the Prevention of
Cruelty to Animals**
www.aspca.org

Tips on planting, insects, and gardening:
**Ohio State Extension**
www.ohioline.osu.edu

## Tools and Supplies

Garden trowel:
**Radius Garden**
www.radiusgarden.com

Diverter kit for rain barrels:
**Garden Water Saver**
http://gardenwatersaver.com

My favorite place to order seeds:
**Johnny's Selected Seeds**
www.johnnyseeds.com

My favorite place to order perennials:
**Bluestone Perennials**
www.bluestoneperennials.com

Miniatures and craft items:
**Pat Catan's Craft Centers**
www.patcatans.com

# * ABOUT THE AUTHOR *

As the Vice President of Education, Renata Fossen Brown oversees the thousands of school children visiting Cleveland Botanical Garden yearly, the development and implementation of teacher professional development workshops, the library, Hershey Children's Garden, and the garden's urban youth farming program, Green Corps. She assisted in the planning and facilitating of a ten-day teacher workshop in Costa Rica to study biodiversity. Brown is involved in the writing of interpretation and exhibit graphics at the garden and served as president of the Cleveland Regional Council of Science Teachers.

Brown holds a B.A. in biology from the University of Toledo and an M.A. in curriculum and instruction from Bradley University, in Peoria, Ill. She is certified to teach grades seven through twelve science, and has been active in informal science education since 1993.

As Assistant Curator of Education at the Toledo Zoo, Brown was responsible for all educational programs occurring on zoo grounds, as well as researching and writing for the zoo's Emmy award-winning television show, *Zoo Today*. Creating and implementing its very first Earth Day celebration is a task of which she is particularly proud. She continued her education role, while adding volunteer coordinator duties and working at Luthy Botanical Garden in Peoria.

A native Clevelander, Renata Fossen Brown gladly returned home in 2004 after a fifteen-year absence. She was named the garden's Clara DeMallie Sherwin Chair in Education in December 2004. She is usually surrounded in her yard by her three dogs and prefers natives and perennials over annuals any day. She is particularly in love with purple coneflower.

**www.cbgarden.org**

# * ACKNOWLEDGMENTS *

Most importantly, thank you to all of my friends and neighbors who let me borrow their children for the creation of this book. Every single one of them amazed me and cracked me up.

To the staff of Cleveland Botanical Garden for giving advice, answering questions, and allowing me the opportunity to write this book, I thank you. Natalie, Ann, Larry, Kathryn, and Geri: Thank you for your support and wisdom.

Many thanks to the Cuyahoga County Soil and Water Conservation District for the hundreds of rain barrels they get out into the community each year!

To the ladies of the Western Reserve Herb Society—you're fantastic and you gave me great ideas, along with a chuckle or two.

To Mary Ann Hall at Quarry Books—thank you for looking me up and giving me such a great opportunity. Your personality made this whole process quite wonderful.

Finally to my husband Dave, who named tools and equipment and gadgets for me, bounced ideas around, walked the dogs when I needed to work, and took absolutely fantastic pictures. Thank you for your patience and support.